W9-AEX-980

Buddha Doodles

Buddha Doodles

Imagine the Possibilities

Molly Hahn

Andrews McMeel
Publishing®

Kansas City • Sydney • London

Start with Love.

Love in such a way
that the person you LOVE
feels free.
— tHicH Nhat hanh

You can't stop the
waves, but you
can learn to surf.

Fill your mind with compassion.

- Buddha

Let yourself be silently drawn by
the strange pull of what you really love.
It will not lead you astray.
—Rumi

Enjoy rituals of pleasure.

Be where
you are.

Dive in and go deep.

Connect to abundance.

Lean toward the light.

Do what makes
you feel alive.

Be light.

You are loved & supported.

Remembering a wrong is like
carrying a burden on the mind.

~Buddha

Absolute attention is prayer.

—Zen Proverb

With our thoughts,
We make the world.

Honor your resilience.

Be kind whenever possible.
It is always possible.

-Dalai Lama

Say hello with love.

May all
beings be
happy & free.

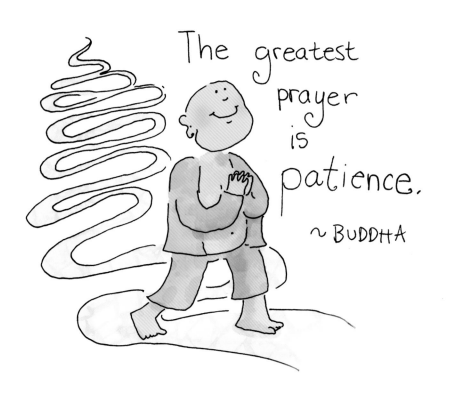

The greatest prayer is patience.

~ BUDDHA

Zen out.

Each moment is yours
to create.

Surrender to
wonder and mystery.

Every heart breaks
so it can let more light in.

Deep within each of us is
a magical jewel that cannot be
scratched, no matter the difficulties.
It is the source of healing,
joy, and wisdom.

May you be joyful
& free toward yourself
& others.

Let a smile spread
through your heart.

Live for peace.

Go with the flow.

simple pleasures

Zen is not some Kind of excitement,
but Concentration on our usual everyday routine.

-Shunryu Suzuki

Create Sacred space.

The words you speak
become the house you
live in.

— Hafiz

Bring Love into each Step.

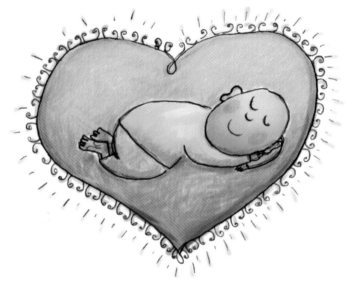

Compassion is always
here for you, waiting
to be
awakened.

Change your perspective.

Be breathed. Be breathed.

The clouds will
always part.

24 brand new hours!

No snowflake ever
falls in the wrong place.

Buddha is inside you.

Give yourself permission
to wander.

Your happiness serves
the world.

Give thanks for your
meal and company.

Listen for mother nature's Love song.

Go forth with strength
and sparkle.

Do things that nourish your soul.

You are precious.

Thousands of candles can be lit
from a single candle, and the life of
the candle will not be shortened.
Happiness never decreases by being shared.
-Buddha

Each small task is
part of life's dance.

Honor transitions.

The best
medicine.

The spirit never ages.

Develop habits that
support a positive attitude.

Be
water.

We are deeply interconnected.

This too shall pass.

Look for Signs.

Make friends with
the unknown.

When you do things from
your soul, you
feel a river moving in you,
a joy.

—Rumi

Silence is the
deepest sound.

Tonight, the moon kisses the stars.
~Rumi

Fill perceptions of lack with LOVE!

Move slowly with Love.

Make time for play.

Be cradled.

Make space.

Revel in the daily
miracles of life.

Embrace joy.
Let go of guilt.

Obstacles are opportunities
for new adventures.

Keep shining your light.

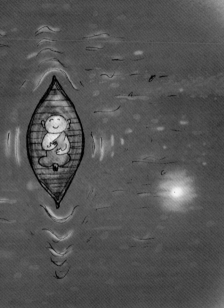

Release.

Soften into your heart.

Keep Letting
Go.

Receive.

Be generous.

Ground.

Care for each
precious moment.

Leave sparks wherever
you go.

Through darkness,
we find light.

Do the work.

Make space
to listen
to your inner
wise voice.

Rest.

It's the simple things that
make you feel at home.

A shadow says that
"Light is here."

We're all just walking
each other home.

~Ram Dass

Andrews McMeel Publishing, LLC
an Andrews McMeel Universal company
1130 Walnut Street, Kansas City, Missouri 64106

www.andrewsmcmeel.com

15 16 17 18 19 TEN 10 9 8 7 6 5 4 3 2 1

ISBN: 978-1-4494-7176-7

Library of Congress Control Number: 2015946041

Editor: Grace Suh
Art director and designer: Julie Barnes
Production editor: Erika Kuster
Production manager: Tamara Haus

ATTENTION: SCHOOLS AND BUSINESSES
Andrews McMeel books are available at quantity discounts with bulk purchase for educational, business, or sales promotional use. For information, please e-mail the Andrews McMeel Publishing Special Sales Department: specialsales@amuniversal.com.